values
ORIENTATION IN SCHOOLS

Johnnie McFadden, Ph.D.
Associate Professor-Assistant Dean
College of Education
University of South Carolina

Joseph C. Rotter, Ed.D.
Associate Professor-G.E. Institute Director
College of Education
University of South Carolina

CENTURY TWENTY ONE PUBLISHING

PUBLISHED BY

**CENTURY TWENTY ONE PUBLISHING
POST OFFICE BOX 8
SARATOGA, CALIFORNIA 95070**

LIBRARY OF CONGRESS CARD CATALOG NUMBER

80-69238

I.S.B.N.

0-86548-045-1

TABLE OF CONTENTS

INTRODUCTION

The purpose of this book emerged from an observable need for children at the middle school/junior high school level to express their values freely and openly, to experience their values, and to receive encouragement as individuals in homes, schools, and communities. Value, as applied in this publication, refers to any characteristic which has psychological, social, moral, or aesthetic importance to the individual. In the plural sense, values reflect a system of beliefs held by the individual which provides for a means of personal security.

The activities which follow are designed in such a way as to help the child systematically look at self, others, and the living environment. Research has shown that, as people become more familiar with themselves, with the people around them, and with their surroundings, they begin to develop more self-reliance, self-motivation, and self-discipline.

The activities are presented so that students are gradually encouraged to assume higher risks and to engage in more self-exploration. The initial activities are oriented with references to objects as they relate to self. For example, within the first section of the book, the activities progress from an external, less threatening approach to those which are internal and more highly personalized. The purpose in presenting the material in this manner is gradually to introduce the students to themselves through a non-threatening approach and to help them develop trust in each other, thus avoiding unfounded value judgements. The teacher or counselor, therefore, is encouraged to follow the activities in the order of their presentation in the manual for most effective

use. However, it is recommended that not more than one activity be covered in one sitting.

In addition to values exploration, several activities provide an opportunity for students to begin to explore careers. Likewise, other activities lend themselves readily to the language arts and social studies curriculum. This publication is not intended for use as an instrument for gathering information for external diagnosis and prescription. Instead, it is written as a tool for students to understand themselves better and to explore expanded dimensions to their value structure.

Values and Me

SUPER HEROES

OBJECTIVE: To identify those personal qualities deemed significant to the
               individual. Through safe external means students are able to
               identify and share certain personal characteristics of importance
               to them.

GROUP: Individually and in small groups of 4 or 5 students

TIME: Thirty minutes

MATERIALS: Comic books, paper and pencil

PROCEDURES: 1. Ask students in advance to bring comic books to school or
                   bring some of your own.

               2. Based on the latest interest in comic books and the "Super
                   Heroes" characters, ask the students to select their favorite
                   super hero.

               3. Have the students to indicate what it is that interests them
                   about the character, i.e., size, sex, color, special skills,
                   etc.

               4. Encourage the students to share their choices in groups of
                   4 or 5.

               5. Then ask each student to create a super-super hero, one with
                   all the qualities they themselves would like to see.

               6. Again, have students share their creations in small groups
                   of 4 or 5 students.

Questions to be asked during small group sharing might include the following:

               1. What are the important traits about the super hero which you
                   chose?

               2. What do you like best about the super hero?

4

3. What do you like least about the super hero?

4. What would you change about the super hero?

5. How do you feel about the super hero you have chosen?

6. In what way is the super hero like you?

7. In what way is the super hero unlike you?

THIS IS ME

OBJECTIVE: To allow the students to take a look at themselves and what
              they value.

              To be able to express these values without fear of judgement by
              their peers.

GROUP: Individually

TIME: Fifteen to twenty minutes

MATERIALS: "This Is Me" form and pencil

PROCEDURES: 1. Each student is asked to complete the "This Is Me" form.

              2. Explain to the students that what they write will be theirs
                  and no one will have access to it but them. To protect con-
                  fidentiality the teacher can provide a central file for safe-
                  keeping. Children may change their form at any time they de-
                  sire.

THIS IS ME

I. "This is me. . ."

    A. My name is _____.

    B. My favorite thing is _____.

    C. My friends say that I am _____.

    D. I think I am _____ _____.

    E. The people _____.

    F. When I a _____.

    G. After sch _____.

    H. My room is _____.

    I. The most impo _____ life is _____.

    J. The most impor _____ fe _____.

    K. I would like to _____.

    L. I like to _____ _____.

    M. I do not like to _____.

II. Here are some important things about me from my past. . .

    A.

    B.

    C.

III. Here are some important things about me <u>now</u>. . .

       A.

       B.

       C.

IV. Here are some important things about my <u>future</u>. . .

       A.

       B.

       C.

_____
                  Date Completed

SELF-DIRECTED BEHAVIOR

OBJECTIVE: To help the students identify their own constructive and destruc-
              tive behaviors. To help the students see that only they can be
              responsible for their own behavior.

GROUP: Small groups of 4 or 5 students

TIME: Thirty minutes

MATERIALS: "OK-Not OK" form and pencils

PROCEDURES: 1. Divide class into groups of 4 or 5 students per group.

              2. Ask students to talk about a typical day including such
                  questions as:

                  What happens?
                  How do I feel when certain things happen?
                  How do others react?

              3. Ask the students to use the "OK-Not OK" form to list in column
                  one thing that happens during the day.

              4. Have the students choose one or two of the OK items and, in
                  column two of the "OK-Not OK" form, list what it is that makes
                  it OK.

              5. Then have the students choose one or two of the Not-OK items
                  and, also in column two of the "OK-Not OK" form, list what it
                  is that makes it Not OK.

              6. Using column three of the form ask the students to think about
                  and write possible solutions to the Not OK items.

              7. In groups of 4 or 5 students ask each participant to share an
                  OK item and a Not OK item. For the Not OK item, ask the student
                  to share what makes it Not OK and any possible solutions, if
                  available. Other students can then share their ideas about how
                  the other student might solve the problem.

9

	1	2	3
Things that help me during the day and what makes it OK	"OK" Things	What makes it OK	How can I keep it OK
Things that get in the way during the day and are Not OK	"Not OK" Things	What makes it Not-OK	What can I do to change it from being Not-OK

WHAT I CAN BE

OBJECTIVE: To help students to take what they have learned about themselves
              and to make some predictions about the future.

GROUP: Individually and total class discussion

TIME: Twenty to thirty minutes

MATERIALS: "What I Can Be" matrix and pencil

PROCEDURES: 1. Ask each student to complete the "What I Can Be" matrix allowing
                 approximately ten minutes for this activity. Ask students to
                 add their own items to each list.

              2. Open class discussion around the "What I Can Be" matrix. The
                 following questions might help in generating ideas from the
                 group:

                 Would someone care to share some likes and dislikes?
                 How do some of the things you like about what you can do differ
                 from some of those things you might do if you were able?
                 How are some of the things you can do like the things you might
                 be?
                 How do you feel about what you think you can be?

              3. Have students file for their future references the completed
                 matrix with the "This Is Me" and "OK-Not OK" forms.

Part I   "What I Can Be"

What I Do	Like very much	Like sometimes	Dislike
1. Go to school			
2. Listen to records			
3. Play sports			
4. Belong to a club			
5. Go to the movies			
6. Have a job			
7. Visit my relatives			
8. Help around the house			
9. Watch TV			
10. Talk with other students			
11. Read books			
12. Spend a lot of time in my room			
13. Go to parties			
14. Go to church			
15. Make things for myself			
16. Make things for others			
17. Do homework			
18. Go shopping			
19. Travel			
20. Ride my bike			
21. Others _____ _____			
_____			
_____			

Part II   "What I Can Be"

What I Can Be or Do	Like very much	Like sometimes	Dislike
1. An important person			
2. Run a business			
3. Make many decisions			
4. Work for other people			
5. Help other people			
6. Make things			
7. Destroy things			
8. A religious person			
9. Handle a lot of money			
10. Work indoors			
11. Get a lot of education			
12. Entertain others			
13. Create things			
14. Spend money			
15. A parent			
16. Work outdoors			
17. Teach people			
18. Organize things			
19. Protect people			
20. Repair things			
21. Others _____			
_____			
_____			

Values and Others

VALUES FOR ME OR FOR YOU

OBJECTIVE: To determine which values belong to oneself and which values
              are others'.

GROUP: Varying number as determined by group leader

MATERIALS: Pencils and "Values for Me or for You" sheet

TIME: Approximately thirty minutes

PROCEDURE: 1. Discuss purposes of this exercise with the group.

              2. Deliver brief lecturette, approximately five minutes on
                 "What Are Values."

              3. Distribute a "Values for Me or for You" sheet to each
                 participant.

              4. Be sure that each person understands the directions and is
                 given adequate time to complete the form.

              5. Divide the total group into several small subgroups, approx-
                 imately 6-8 persons, and encourage them to share the contents
                 of their form individually.

              6. Request participants in groups to compile their results in
                 order to determine the degree of consensus among them.

              7. Evaluate process and content of activity with total group.

VALUES FOR ME OR FOR YOU

Directions: Read the following topics and code them in conjunction with your value system. - "M" for those values which are important to you; "O" for those values which are important to others; "B" for those values which you consider to be important both to yourself and to others.

_____Reading		_____Politics
_____Exercise		_____Travel
_____Education		_____Biking
_____Money		_____Sleeping
_____People		_____Eating
_____Singing		_____Children
_____Poetry		_____Parents
_____Science		_____Relatives
_____Sports		_____Teachers
_____Friendship		_____Doctors
_____Flying		_____Shopping
_____Helping Others		_____Patriotism
_____Clothes		_____Nature
_____Work		_____Television
_____Religion		_____Radio
_____Time		_____Leisure time
_____Food		_____Grooming
_____Weight Control		_____Leadership
_____Health		_____Talking
_____Love		_____Success

PRIORITY OF VALUES

OBJECTIVE: To study the priority of values for oneself, one's family, and one's peers.

GROUP: Small groups ranging from 5-10 in size

MATERIALS: Pencils and "Ordering Values" sheet

TIME: Approximately forty-five minutes

PROCEDURE: 1. Arrange participants in small groups, 5-10 persons per group.

2. Explain purpose of this activity with participating individuals.

3. Distribute an "Ordering Values" sheet to each participant.

4. Provide the group with a clear explanation of how to use the grid on the "Ordering Values" sheet.

5. Have participants to complete the grid individually.

6. Request participants to exchange sheets with each other within their small group for review.

7. Ask participants to summarize what they learned about each other's value system after studying the sheet of their peers.

8. Allow persons who initiated information on their grids to confirm or to modify statements of interpretation offered by peers within the small group.

ORDERING VALUES

Directions: Read the values below and check corresponding columns for you and
others. Then order the list of values for you by placing numerals
from 1 to 20 on the blank lines. "1" means most important and "20"
means least important.

Value	Mine	Parents		Siblings				Friends			
		His	Hers	1 His	2 His	1 Hers	2 Hers	1 His	2 His	1 Hers	2 Hers
A___ Choosing a friend											
B___ Visiting a bakery											
C___ Making people happy											
D___ Reading books											
E___ Being self-disciplined											
F___ Learning new skills											
G___ Winning the game											
H___ Taking photographs											
I___ Earning good grades											
J___ Making choices											
K___ Influencing others											
L___ Thinking for one's self											
M___ Viewing television											
N___ Eating ice cream											
O___ Keeping a diary											
P___ Delivering a speech											
Q___ Giving a gift											
R___ Writing letters											
S___ Listening to suggestions											
T___ Getting along with parents											

WHEEL OF VALUES

OBJECTIVE: To analyze one's interpretation of values maintained by others within one's personal and community life space.

GROUP: Maximum of twenty-four participants

MATERIALS: Numbered chips (24), "Wheel of Values" sheet, and pencils

TIME: Approximately one hour

PROCEDURE: 1. Distribute one "Wheel of Values" sheet per participant.

2. Request each person to select one chip and keep it concealed until later in the exercise.

3. Ask participants to pantomime the character corresponding to his/her chip and wait for another participant to identify accurately three values of importance to the character being portrayed. The pantomimist confirms or rejects the values being related about his/her character. The participant guessing the values must have at least two out of three confirmed by the pantomimist before he/she earns privilege to portray the character for his/her chip.

4. Ask each pantomimist to keep a record of the final guesses of values which he/she confirms for his/her character.

5. Collect written values in final form from each participant.

6. Compile list of values to correspond with each character for distribution and discussion at a subsequent discussion session. The facilitator of this value activity is responsible for a follow-up discussion on comparison of values for corresponding characters and participants.

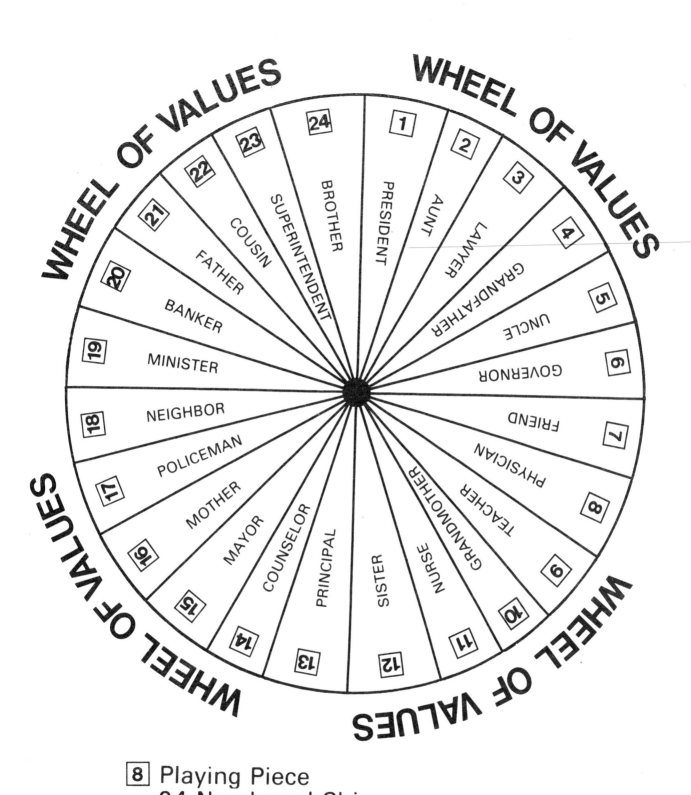

⬚8 Playing Piece
24 Numbered Chips

OTHERS AROUND ME

OBJECTIVE: To review activities which appear to have special meaning to
              persons around oneself.

GROUP: 20-25 participants

MATERIALS: Pencils and "Identity and Values" form

TIME: Approximately forty-five minutes

PROCEDURE: 1. Relate purpose of this activity with the participants.

              2. Distribute "Identity and Values" form to each participant.

              3. Explain meaning of directions for the form to everyone and
                  entertain questions.

              4. Request students to complete the form carefully.

              5. Ask students to assemble into small groups, approximately five
                  each, and discuss common aspects of their written responses.
                  Encourage students to indicate behaviors which they have ob-
                  served that provided them with clues for their common responses.

              6. Provide the total group with a summary of the exercise and key
                  concepts which were learned.

IDENTITY AND VALUES

Directions: Read the following statements and write the names of person(s) in your class who are <u>most</u> associated with each description. The same name may appear on more than one line.

_____ 1. Someone who is a serious student.

_____ 2. Someone who is a good athlete.

_____ 3. Someone who speaks with a clear voice.

_____ 4. Someone who wears glasses.

_____ 5. Someone who eats heartily.

_____ 6. Someone who is very dependable.

_____ 7. Someone who plays a musical instrument.

_____ 8. Someone who reads often.

_____ 9. Someone who sings with a choir.

_____ 10. Someone who speaks another language.

_____ 11. Someone who has brothers and sisters.

_____ 12. Someone who has been on television.

_____ 13. Someone who knows how to roller skate.

_____ 14. Someone who enjoys animals.

_____ 15. Someone who knows plants.

_____ 16. Someone who is a quiet person.

_____ 17. Someone who has moved to the neighborhood recently.

_____ 18. Someone who has been on a vacation.

_____ 19. Someone who is a scout.

_____ 20. Someone who likes people.

_____ 21. Someone who knows the subject of mathematics.

_____ 22. Someone who draws well.

_____ 23. Someone who is a helper of others.

_____ 24. Someone who has visited the state capitol.

_____ 25. Someone who enjoys freedom.

A CURVE OF VALUES

OBJECTIVE: To analyze value profiles of oneself, one's closest peer, and the individual with whom one has the greatest social distance.

GROUP: Small subgroups, ranging 6-8 persons each, within the total class.

MATERIALS: Pencils and "Value Profiles" graph form

TIME: Approximately thirty minutes

PROCEDURE: 1. Explain the meaning of drawing profiles, reinforcing technical aspects of a line graph.

               2. Circulate "Value Profiles" forms and answer questions for further clarification.

               3. Ask participants to plot corresponding points on the form and complete line graph for the following persons:

                          Oneself
                          Closest Peer
                          Most Socially Distant

               4. Permit participants sufficient time to study interrelationships among persons plotted on the graph and their significance.

               5. Allow time for open discussion within the total group.

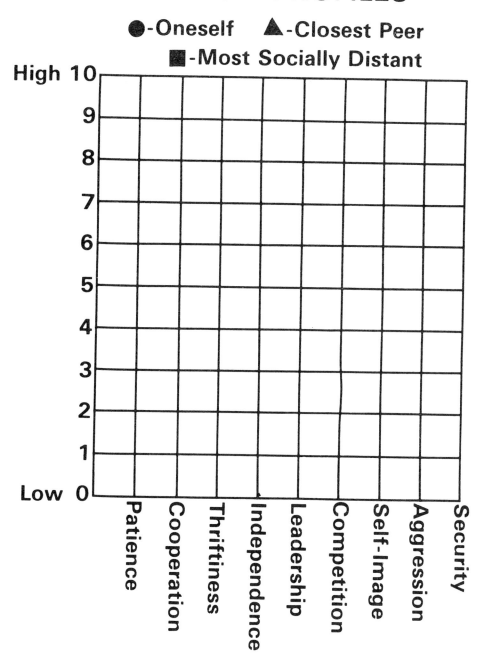

VALUE PROFILES

●-Oneself ▲-Closest Peer

■-Most Socially Distant

High 10

9

8

7

6

5

4

3

2

1

Low 0

Patience Cooperation Thriftiness Independence Leadership Competition Self-Image Aggression Security

Values and Environment

VALUING ON LOCATION

OBJECTIVE: To study the emergence of values through places frequented.

GROUP: Range of 10-15 participants

MATERIALS: "Value Squares" sheet per individual or "Value Squares" poster per group and a set of chips

TIME: Approximately forty-five minutes

PROCEDURE:

1. Provide each group with a "Value Squares" poster or sheet and a set of chips. Single chips contain one alphabet each to correspond with those shown on the "Value Squares" poster or sheet.

2. Have participant to shake chips in a container and request each person to select an alphabet from the container. Participants should select a chip only when their time to respond occurs.

3. Ask each person to answer the following questions for the place that corresponds with his/her chosen chip (alphabet):

   a. What do you recall of your earliest experiences here?

   b. What do you like or dislike about the place represented on your chip?

   c. What is the specific location of your favorite place shown on your chip?

   d. What values have you derived from the place shown?

   e. What careers can you name for your chip that would have some appeal for you?

4. Ask participants in each subgroup to summarize values on which they can attain consensus to depict values that they value as related to places on the "Value Squares" poster or sheet.

5. Note that other places can be substituted for those listed on the form following this page.

A	N	D	J	W
Q	H	O	U	K
F	R	B	P	E
L	V	S	I	Y
X	M	G	T	C

A	Playing Piece

KEY

A. Church
B. Highway
C. Library
D. Park
E. Automobile
F. Theater
G. Bus
H. Athletic Field
I. Drugstore
J. Airplane
K. Ice Cream Parlor
L. School
M. Train

N. Museum
O. Taxi
P. Grocery Store
Q. Campground
R. Sandwich Shop
S. Coliseum
T. Bicycle
U. Physician's Office
V. Restaurant
W. Florist
X. Hotel
Y. Newsstand

SEEING IS BELIEVING

OBJECTIVE: To review television programs and their influences on shaping value systems.

GROUP: 15-25 participants

MATERIALS: Pencils and "TV-Seeing Is Believing" form

TIME: Approximately forty-five minutes

PROCEDURE:
1. Ask the total group to render verbal responses to their interpretation of the expression, "Seeing Is Believing."

2. Divide participants into small groups, approximately 7-10 persons per group.

3. Distribute one copy of the "TV-Seeing Is Believing" form to each participant.

4. Request every person to complete the form individually.

5. Have participants to discuss their recorded material with their small group members. Helpful questions related to values within the group should be encouraged.

6. Solicit a brief verbal report from each subgroup for summarizing purposes.

TV-SEEING IS BELIEVING

Directions: Use this form to accompany the exercise, "Seeing Is Believing".
Additional procedures will be given to you by your group leader.

I. Identify your three most favorite television programs.

   A. First choice _____

   B. Second choice_____

   C. Third choice _____

II. List your key personality in each program and traits for each person which
are most appealing to you.

TELEVISION PROGRAM   KEY PERSONALITY   APPEALING TRAITS

                                                      A._____
A. _____   A. _____
                                                      A._____

                                                      B._____
B. _____   B. _____
                                                      B._____

                                                      C._____
C. _____   C. _____
                                                      C._____

III. Record aspects of each program that you would retain.

   _____

   _____

   _____

IV. Write ways by which you feel that you have been influenced by each program.

   _____

   _____

   _____

READING THE HEADLINES

OBJECTIVE: To explore individual values which are influenced by environmental forces reported through the written page.

GROUP: Varying number to be determined by the group facilitator

MATERIALS: Pencils, paper, and "Headlines" sheet

TIME: Approximately one hour

PROCEDURE:
1. Discuss the meaning of headlines with students.

2. Distribute one "Headlines" sheet to each participant and explain that the topics reflect real stories which appeared in newspapers.

3. Ask students to follow the directions on their "Headlines" sheet.

4. Form groups of approximately five persons each.

5. Request participants individually to write a brief story about the "number one" headline on his/her list.

6. Have participants to read their story and have their small group members to react.

7. Tell students to cluster the headlines into five groupings, i.e., in clusters from most to least significance (A-B-C-D-E) to represent the thinking of their subgroup.

8. Allow students time to develop a series of news flashes for any one cluster to represent their group.

9. Read news flashes to the total group.

ALTERNATE ACTIVITY:

1. Ask students individually to select the word which initially captures their attention from each of the topics from the "Headlines" sheet.

2. Have students to write a sentence for each word selected. Words identified by each student may be clustered in sentences.

3. Select sentences from students, write them on the chalkboard with blank lines for key words, and request students to complete the blanks and to explain their interpretation of the given sentence.

HEADLINES

Directions: Read each of the twenty-five headlines and rank them in order from 1 (most important) to 25 (least important), indicating the order in which you would read the features.

A _____ Workers Shift away from Ford

B _____ Exemption Sought from School Fees

C _____ A Million Can't Quell Barbara's Fear That She'll Fail

D _____ Test Says Johnny Can Read Better

E _____ The Case against Nixon

F _____ Soviets Say Saturn's Rings Actually Rainbows

G _____ Rage and Fear in South Africa

H _____ After the Debate: Key Questions Remain

I _____ Saturday's Last Day for Voter Registration

J _____ Police Chiefs See End to Control by 'Liberals'

K _____ 2.5 Million More Americans in Poverty

L _____ A Taxing Divorce: Dividing the Profits

M _____ Toys Teach

N _____ Rhodesia Plan Gets Black Veto

O _____ Carter's Wife Favors Easing of Pot Laws

P _____ Kidnapped Wife Found Tied to Tree

Q _____ Women's Ordination OK Saddens Charlotte Priest

R _____ Open Assassination Probe Sought

S _____ New Bike Route Unsafe, Club Leader Charges

T _____ Someone Else Is Champ

U _____ Hearst Is Given Seven Years

V _____ Food Quiz

W _____ New Speedometers Stop at 85 MPH

X _____ National Health Insurance Still a Dream

Y _____ Schools Must Serve All

JOURNEY TO A STAR

OBJECTIVES: To help students to recognize those values which they cherish and
              to aid them in developing decision-making skills.
              To give them experience with the dilemmas which people face when
              they are forced to make decisions.
              To show that value differences exist among people, but that through
              consensus group decisions can be made.

GROUP: Individually, in groups of 4 or 5 students, and total class

TIME: Forty-five minutes

MATERIALS: Newsprint pad and magic marker or crayons

PROCEDURES: 1. Each student is given a copy of the "Journey to a Star" story
                  with directions and the survival lists.

              2. Each student, after reading the story, chooses the 8 items
                  and persons to remain with the ship.

              3. Students are asked to form groups of 4 or 5 members. Groups
                  may be formed by several methods. One approach is to take
                  the total number of students, divide by the number of desired
                  per group, then ask students to count off by the arrived figure;
                  e.g., if there are 30 students in the group and you desire 5
                  students per group, then divide 5 into 30 to get 6. The students
                  count off from 1 to 6, thus forming 6 groups of 5 students each.

              4. Each group arrives at an agreed-upon list of items and personnel
                  through consensus.

              5. A representative (chosen within each group) from each group then
                  reports his/her group's decisions to the total class.

              6. Differences are then discussed by the total class.

JOURNEY TO A STAR

Directions to Students and Story:

You are the captain of the crew on a space shuttle traveling to a distant galaxy. Enroute to your destination your space shuttle encounters mechanical malfunction. Your radio communication system has been destroyed and there is no way to communicate with the home base. In order to safely return home it becomes necessary to lighten your load and, therefore, eject two parts of the ship. The oxygen supply is also low and can only support the lives of 8 of the 10 people aboard for the return trip. Assume that all ship parts weigh the same and that all personnel weigh the same.

1. You are to choose from the list of 10 ship parts the 2 that are to be ejected to lighten the load.

2. Also choose from the list of 10 people the 8 who would return with the ship.

3. Then share your choices with others in your group.

Space Shuttle Parts

1. Subspace Radio

2. Food Preparation System

3. Maintenance Equipment

4. Ship's Computer

5. Ship's Gymnasium

6. Hospital Facility

7. Spare Engine

8. Alternative Power System

9. Gyroscope

10. Ship's Library

SPACE-SHUTTLE PERSONNEL

1. Captain

2. Chaplain

3. Engineer

4. Linguist

5. Electrician

6. Physician

7. Security Officer

8. Politician

9. Scientist

10. Cook

INCOMPLETE SITUATIONS

OBJECTIVE: To help students understand that judgement about others is so often made with limited information.

GROUP: Class

TIME: Twenty to thirty minutes

MATERIALS: None

PROCEDURES: 1. Present situations individually and ask students to conclude from the limited information what is happening.

              2. Discuss differences of opinion.

              3. Ask students to create additional scenes and to react.

              4. Open discussion around how the environment and the amount of information available influences how we are perceived or perceive others.

SITUATIONS

I.   You see your best friend slowly approaching a tavern, then quickly looking around and dashing into the tavern.

II.   You are riding past a church on your bike and suddenly see someone bursting through the doors carrying something shiny and running down the street.

III. A friend of yours says she will meet you after school to talk about a party she is having on Saturday. When you come to see her after school, you find her quickly walking away with another person.

IV.   It is the night of the school dance. You walk in and see the girl/boy who said she/he couldn't go with you because she/he had to do something else but is standing and talking with another boy/girl.

V.   You are walking through the park and see three teenagers standing in the distance by a tree. One is holding a package, another some money. Suddenly two of the teens run off leaving the third behind.

VI.   Develop your own situation.

IF I COULD, I WOULD

OBJECTIVE: To help students understand that the environment within which we
find ourselves often explain our attitudes about many things.

GROUP: Individually and class discussion

TIME: Twenty to thirty minutes

MATERIALS: "If I Could, I Would" form and pencil

PROCEDURES: 1. Ask the students to complete column one of "If I Could, I Would"
Questionnaire. Explain that they may check as many items as
they like.

2. After the students have completed the questionnaire, ask them to
share each item separately. Group the students according to
their answer to item one and make note of the size of each group.

3. Ask students in each group to discuss their commonalities while
also looking for differences.

4. Move to item 2 and proceed as with item 1.

5. On another day, column two can be processed as with column one
with the emphasis on how they would like situations to be.
Notice the difference in groupings.

VARIATIONS: 1. Can be used as a sociometric instrument. How students group
themselves in classroom activities may be reflected in the way
in which they respond to the questionnaire.

2. Students may role play their responses to the questionnaire
and have others guess what they are depicting.

38

3. Students may assume a role different from their own experience, such as one which they would like to hold but presently do not.

4. Students may exchange roles with each other to recognize what it is like to view things from the other person's perspective.

IF I COULD, I WOULD

1. I live in

_____A small house

_____A medium size house

_____A large house

_____An apartment

_____A condominium

2. My house is located in the

_____City

_____Country

_____Suburbs

3. Most of the time I spend time

_____Indoors

_____Outdoors

_____At home

_____Away from home

4. I usually

_____Work with my hands

_____Read

_____Play baseball

_____Play monopoly

1. I would like to live in

_____A small house

_____A medium size house

_____A large house

_____An apartment

_____A condominium

2. I wish my house was located in the

_____City

_____Country

_____Suburbs

3. I would prefer to be

_____Indoors

_____Outdoors

_____At home

_____Away from home

4. I would like to

_____Work with my hands

_____Read

_____Play baseball

_____Play monopoly

5. I have a lot of privacy_____

   I sometimes have privacy_____

   I never have privacy_____

6. I usually am

   _____Alone

   _____With others

7. My family spends a lot of time

   _____Outdoors

   _____Indoors

8. Our vacations are spent

   _____At home

   _____Away from home

9. We travel a lot_____

   We travel very little_____

   We never travel_____

10. When we stay overnight some-
    where, we usually

    _____Camp

    _____Stay in a motel

    _____Stay with friends or
          relatives

5. I would prefer to have

   _____A lot of privacy

   _____Privacy sometimes

   _____No privacy

6. I would prefer to be

   _____Alone

   _____With others

7. I wish my family would spend
   more time

   _____Outdoors

   _____Indoors

8. I wish our vacations were spent

   _____At home

   _____Away from home

9. I would prefer to

   _____Travel a lot

   _____Travel very little

   _____Never travel

10. When we stay overnight some-
    where, I would prefer to

    _____Camp

    _____Stay in a motel

    _____Stay with friends or
          relatives

OTHER TITLES AVAILABLE FROM
CENTURY TWENTY ONE PUBLISHING

NEW DIRECTIONS IN ETHNIC STUDIES: MINORITIES IN AMERICA by David
    Claerbaut, Editor   Perfect Bound   LC# 80-69327
    ISBN 0-86548-025-7 $9.95
COLLECTING, CULTURING, AND CARING FOR LIVING MATERIALS: GUIDE FOR
    TEACHER, STUDENT AND HOBBYIST by William E. Claflin   Perfect
    Bound   LC# 80-69329   ISBN 0-86548-026-5 $8.50
TEACHING ABOUT THE OTHER AMERICANS: MINORITIES IN UNITED STATES
    HISTORY by Ann Curry   Perfect Bound   LC# 80-69120
    ISBN 0-86548-028-1 $8.95
MULTICULTURAL TRANSACTIONS: A WORKBOOK FOCUSING ON COMMUNICATION
    BETWEEN GROUPS by James S. DeLo and William A. Green   Perfect
    Bound   LC# 80-69328   ISBN 0-86548-030-3 $11.50
LEARNING TO TEACH by Richard B. Dierenfield   Perfect Bound
    LC# 80-69119   ISBN 0-86548-031-1 $10.95
LEARNING TO THINK--TO LEARN by M. Ann Dirkes   Perfect Bound
    LC# 80-65613   ISBN 0-86548-032-X $11.50
PLAY IN PRESCHOOL MAINSTREAMED AND HANDICAPPED SETTINGS by Anne Cairns
    Federlein   Perfect Bound   LC# 80-65612   ISBN 0-86548-035-4
    $10.50
THE NATURE OF LEADERSHIP FOR HISPANICS AND OTHER MINORITIES by
    Ernest Yutze Flores   Perfect Bound   LC# 80-69239
    ISBN 0-86548-036-2 $10.95
THE MINI-GUIDE TO LEADERSHIP by Ernest Yutze Flores   Perfect Bound
    LC# 80-83627   ISBN 0-86548-037-0 $5.50
THOUGHTS, TROUBLES AND THINGS ABOUT READING FROM THE CRADLE THROUGH
    GRADE THREE by Carolyn T. Gracenin   Perfect Bound
    LC# 80-65611   ISBN 0-86548-038-9 $14.95
BETWEEN TWO CULTURES: THE VIETNAMESE IN AMERICA by Alan B. Henkin and
    Liem Thanh Nguyen   Perfect Bound   LC# 80-69333
    ISBN 0-86548-039-7 $7.95
PERSONALITY CHARACTERISTICS AND DISCIPLINARY ATTITUDES OF CHILD-
    ABUSING MOTHERS by Alan L. Evans   Perfect Bound   LC# 80-69240
    ISBN 0-86548-033-8 $11.95
PARENTAL EXPECTATIONS AND ATTITUDES ABOUT CHILDREARING IN HIGH RISK
    VS. LOW RISK CHILD ABUSING FAMILIES by Gary C. Rosenblatt
    Perfect Bound   LC# 79-93294   ISBN 0-86548-020-6 $10.00
CHILD ABUSE AS VIEWED BY SUBURBAN ELEMENTARY SCHOOL TEACHERS by David
    A. Pelcovitz   Perfect Bound   LC# 79-93295   ISBN 0-86548-019-2
    $10.00
PHYSICAL CHILD ABUSE: AN EXPANDED ANALYSIS by James R. Seaberg
    Perfect Bound   LC# 79-93293   ISBN 0-86548-021-4 $10.00
THE DISPOSITION OF REPORTED CHILD ABUSE by Marc F. Maden   Perfect
    Bound   LC# 79-93296   ISBN 0-86548-016-8 $10.00
EDUCATIONAL AND PSYCHOLOGICAL PROBLEMS OF ABUSED CHILDREN by James
    Christiansen   Perfect Bound   LC# 79-93303   ISBN 0-86548-003-6
    $10.00
DEPENDENCY, FRUSTRATION TOLERANCE, AND IMPULSE CONTROL IN CHILD ABUSERS
    by Don Kertzman   Perfect Bound   LC# 79-93297   ISBN 86548-015-X
    $10.00
SUCCESSFUL STUDENT TEACHING: A HANDBOOK FOR ELEMENTARY AND SECONDARY
    STUDENT TEACHERS by Fillmer Hevener, Jr.   Perfect Bound
    LC# 80-69332   ISBN 0-86548-040-0 $8.95
BLACK COMMUNICATION IN WHITE SOCIETY by Roy Cogdell and Sybil Wilson
    Perfect Bound   LC# 79-93302   ISBN 0-86548-004-4 $13.00

SCHOOL VANDALISM: CAUSE AND CURE by Robert Bruce Williams and Joseph
    L. Venturini   Perfect Bound   LC# 80-69230   ISBN 0-86548-060-5
    $9.50
LEADERS, LEADING, AND LEADERSHIP by Harold W. Boles   Perfect Bound
    LC# 80-65616   ISBN 0-86548-023-0 $14.95
LEGAL OUTLOOK: A MESSAGE TO COLLEGE AND UNIVERSITY PEOPLE by Ulysses
    V. Spiva   Perfect Bound   LC# 80-69232   ISBN 0-86548-057-5
    $9.95
THE NAKED CHILD THE LONG RANGE EFFECTS OF FAMILY AND SOCIAL NUDITY
    by Dennis Craig Smith   Perfect Bound   LC# 80-69234
    ISBN 0-86548-056-7 $7.95
SIGNIFICANT INFLUENCE PEOPLE: A SIP OF DISCIPLINE AND ENCOURAGEMENT
    by Joseph C. Rotter, Johnnie McFadden and Gary D. Kannenberg
    Perfect Bound   LC# 80-69233   ISBN 0-86548-055-9 $8.95
LET'S HAVE FUN WITH ENGLISH by Ruth Rackmill   Perfect Bound
    LC# 80-68407   ISBN 0-86548-061-3 $6.95
CHILDREN'S PERCEPTIONS OF ELDERLY PERSONS by Lillian A. Phenice
    Perfect Bound   LC# 80-65604   ISBN 0-86548-054-0 $10.50
URBAN EDUCATION: AN ANNOTATED BIBLIOGRAPHY by Arnold G. Parks
    Perfect Bound   LC# 80-69234   ISBN 0-86548-053-2 $9.50
DYNAMICS OF CLASSROOM STRUCTURE by Charles J. Nier   Perfect Bound
    LC# 80-69330   ISBN 0-86548-052-4 $11.50
SOCIOLOGY IN BONDAGE: AN INTRODUCTION TO GRADUATE STUDY by Harold A.
    Nelson   Perfect Bound   LC# 80-65605   ISBN 0-86548-051-6 $9.95
BEYOND THE OPEN CLASSROOM: TOWARD INFORMAL EDUCATION by Lorraine L.
    Morgan, Vivien C. Richman and Ann Baldwin Taylor   Perfect Bound
    LC# 80-69235   ISBN 0-86548-050-8 $9.50
INTRODUCTORY SOCIOLOGY: LECTURES, READINGS AND EXERCISES by Gordon D.
    Morgan   Perfect Bound   LC# 80-65606   ISBN 0-86548-049-4
    $10.50
THE STUDENT TEACHER ON THE FIRING LINE by D. Eugene Meyer   Perfect
    Bound   LC# 80-69236   ISBN 0-86548-048-6 $11.95
VALUES ORIENTATION IN SCHOOL by Johnnie McFadden and Joseph C. Rotter
    Perfect Bound   LC# 80-69238   ISBN 0-86548-045-1 $4.50
MOVEMENT THEMES: TOPICS FOR EARLY CHILDHOOD LEARNING THROUGH CREATIVE
    MOVEMENT by Barbara Stewart Jones   Perfect Bound   LC# 80-65608
    ISBN 0-86548-042-7 $8.50
FROM BIRTH TO TWELVE: HOW TO BE A SUCCESSFUL PARENT TO INFANTS AND
    CHILDREN by Gary D. Kannenberg   Perfect Bound   LC# 80-69331
    ISBN 0-86548-043-5 $7.95

4816

A